JAN 1 3 2011

My Country

Ellen K. Mitten

ROURKE PUBLISHING
www.rourkepublishing.com

www.rourkepublishing.com

PHOTO CREDITS: Cover: © gisele; Title Page: © Neil Johnston; Page 3, 5: © Natural_Warp; Page 9: © Joseph C. Justice Jr.; Page 11, 15: © Wikipedia; Page 13: © Lisa F. Young; Page 17: © Aaron Kohr; Page 19: © Daniel LaFlor; Page 20: © Keith Reicher; Page 21: © Nick Schlax; Page 22: © Natural_Warp, © Daniel LaFlor; Page 23: © Wikipedia, © Lisa F. Young

Edited by Meg Greve

Cover design by Renee Brady
Interior design by Tara Raymo

Library of Congress Cataloging-in-Publication Data

Mitten, Ellen K.
 My country / Ellen K. Mitten.
   p. cm. -- (Little world social studies)
 Includes bibliographical references and index.
 ISBN 978-1-61590-328-3 (Hard Cover) (alk. paper)
 ISBN 978-1-61590-567-6 (Soft Cover)
 1. United States--Juvenile literature. I. Title.
 E178.3.M69 2011
 973--dc22
                            2010009264

Rourke Publishing
Printed in the United States of America, North Mankato, Minnesota
033010
033010LP

www.rourkepublishing.com - rourke@rourkepublishing.com
Post Office Box 643328 Vero Beach, Florida 32964

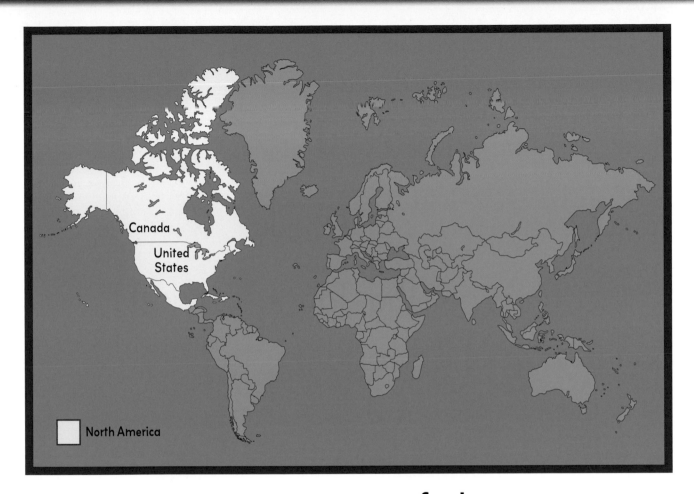

My **country** is part of the
continent of North America.

My country is the fourth largest country in the world.

Russia - 1st Largest

China - 3rd Largest

Canada - 2nd Largest

United States - 4th Largest

My country, the United States of America, is made up of 50 states.

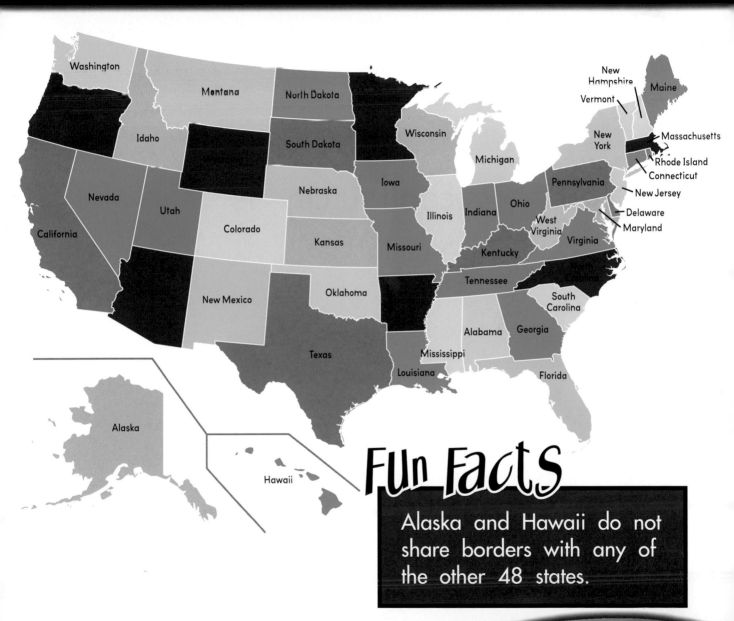

Fun Facts

Alaska and Hawaii do not share borders with any of the other 48 states.

My country's capital city is Washington, D.C.

FuN FactS

The president lives in the White House in Washington, D.C.

My country's **government** is a democracy.

In a democracy, people **vote** for their leaders.

Fun Facts

If you are a citizen of the United States and 18 years old, you have the right to vote.

Every four years, the citizens of my country vote for the person they want to be the **president**.

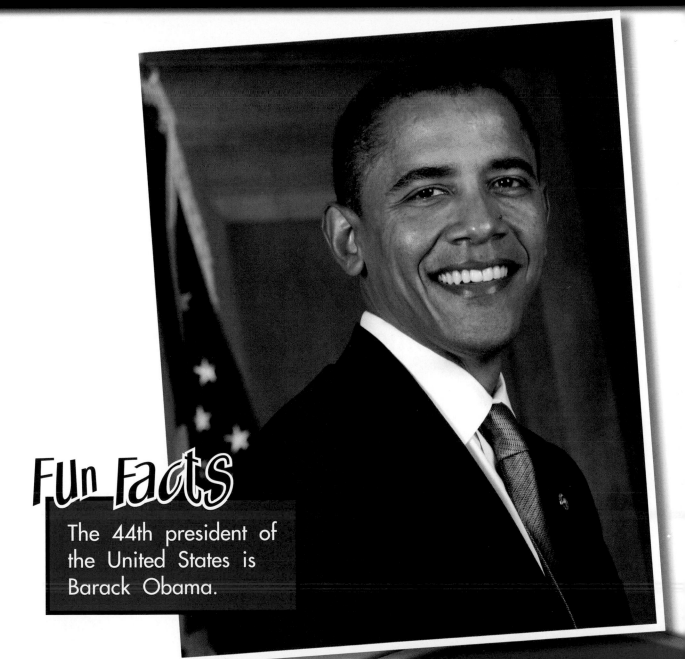

Fun Facts

The 44th president of the United States is Barack Obama.

My country has many people in it. Over 300 million people live in my country.

People from all different backgrounds are Americans. My country is a place of great **diversity**.

My country has many things to see and do. My country, the United States of America, is a great place to live!

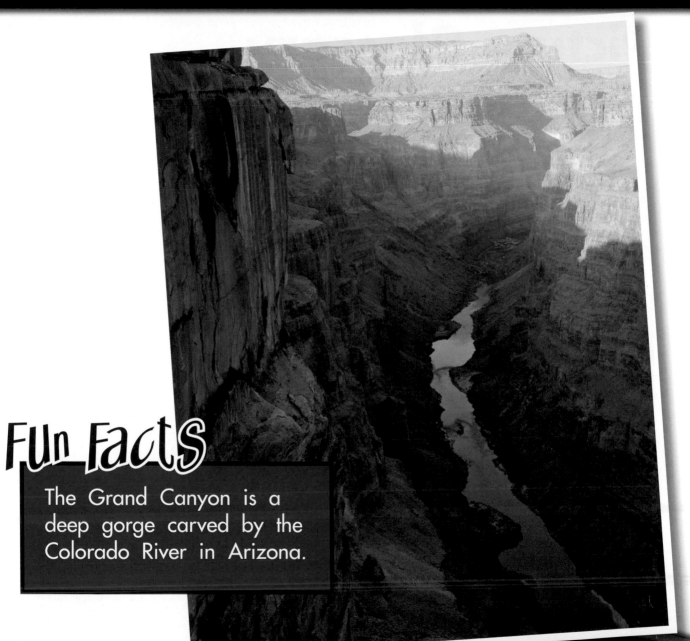

FUn FactS

The Grand Canyon is a deep gorge carved by the Colorado River in Arizona.

Picture Glossary

 **continent** (KON-tuh-nuht): A large landmass. The seven continents on Earth are Asia, Africa, Europe, North America, South America, Australia, and Antarctica.

 **country** (KUHN-tree): A part of the world with its own borders and government. The United States of America is a country.

 **diversity** (di-VUR-suh-tee): A collection of different things. Diversity in people includes differences in race, religion, and culture.

government (GUHV-urn-muhnt): A group of people who carry out the affairs of a country, state, or organization.

president (PREZ-uh-duhnt): The elected leader or chief executive of a country.

vote (VOHT): To make a choice in an election or other poll.

Index

Websites

About the Author

Ellen K. Mitten has been teaching four and five year-olds since 1995. She and her family love reading all sorts of books!